WRITE YOUR STORY

TURN YOUR LIFE INTO FICTION IN 10 EASY STEPS

HELENA HALME

INTRODUCTION

During my MA in Creative writing some 10 years ago, writing the story of your life was somewhat frowned upon. Yet, one of the most often uttered pieces of advice was to 'write what you know'. I could never marry the two strands of thinking. How are you supposed to write about what you know, but not be allowed to use your life for inspiration?

I did, however, take my MA tutors' advice and after graduating wrote two fictional novels, *Coffee and Vodka*, and *The Red King of Helsinki*. In both novels I used my life as a reference to the time and subject matter of these two stories.

But when, over fifteen years ago, I began my blog, *Helena's London Life*, (now on my site www.helenahalme.com) I was often asked by my readers why I moved to England from my native Finland. So I started a series of posts, telling the story of my life, of how I met and married my English husband. I was imagining that I'd write four or five posts at the most, but when I got to number 25, I realized what I was actually writing was a novel.

You ask – a novel? Surely what you were writing was an autobiography? Yes, well, it started that way, but being that I am a novelist, new plot lines and characters kept infiltrating the story, and about half way through, I decided I'd give in to my novelist tendencies and carry on writing a fictionalized book of the true story.

Doris Lessing wrote in one of her memoirs that we all re-write history and that therefore no autobiography can be an accurate account of events. I found out pretty soon that I was not capable of writing a memoir, even with my own version of the 'truth' so my only choice was to write a fictionalized account of my life. But I thoroughly enjoyed the process. So much so, that I ended up writing a series of Nordic romance books, which follow Kaisa and Peter as they try to navigate in the stormy waters of their multicultural relationship.

So how did I do it – and what is my advice to those wishing to turn their life into a novel?

RESEARCH: GET INSPIRED

I know it sounds crazy to research your own life. You know the details right? But in order to write a story, you need to get those creative juices going. You need to get inspired. You need to dig deep into your emotions and your own, and the other characters', mindsets at that time.

And sometimes, you might have forgotten some vital details. Or you might ignore some interesting snippet from your life that explains the way you and the other characters in your book are feeling.

In order to make your life interesting to your readers, it needs to be an engaging tale. And any good story needs to be researched.

I'd tried to write my story for a long time

The first time I tried to write the story of how I met my Englishman at the British Embassy in Helsinki was for the 'Our Tune' feature of Simon Bates BBC Radio 1 show. If you lived in the UK in the 80s, you cannot have escaped this section of the show where soppy 'true' love stories sent in by the listeners were read out by Simon Bates over Nino Rota's Love Theme from *Romeo and Juliet*. But all my efforts at writing came to nothing because I just didn't know how to tell the story. Up to that point, all I'd written was a diary and news stories at my day job with the BBC. I wasn't equipped with the tools to write a romantic tale and just didn't know where to start.

An Officer and a Gentleman

In 1986, after I'd been married to my Englishman, a British Navy Officer, for a year, I decided to surprise him at Fort Lauderdale. It's a sea port town in Florida that the aircraft carrier, HMS Invincible, which the Englishman was serving on as an Officers' Training Officer, was due to visit. He was a bit taken aback when he spotted me on the quayside as the ship was coming into dock, but that's another story :-).

While in the US, the Englishman wore his tropical uniform most of the time. This was quite a treat for me (I always loved him in uniform) because in the UK the members of the armed forces weren't allowed to wear a uniform in public unless taking part in an official engagement, due to the very real (and scary) IRA terror threat. In the US being in uniform was not only allowed but encouraged.

When out and about, with my handsome officer husband, we had many comments from the locals that we looked just like Richard Gere and Debra Winger from *An Officer and a Gentleman*. The film had come out a couple of years earlier. I didn't think I looked anything like Ms Winger (I was blonde for one!), but when we were kissing goodbye at the airport and a woman wanted to take a photo of us, claiming we were the spitting image of the romantic couple, I began to think there must be something in it. But I forgot all about it when I boarded the plane to fly home – alone – feeling the very real pain of yet another separation.

Robert McKee Story Seminar

Years later, with an MA in Creative Writing, and a novel, *Coffee and Vodka*, under my belt, I decided to take a course called The Story Seminar by Robert McKee. This was a long, and intensive, weekend program in scriptwriting, something I thought I might try to learn. I didn't pursue a career in that direction, but the course changed my idea of writing and story-telling forever. (But that's yet another, different, conversation.) At the end of the course, we dissected the classic film, *Casablanca*, with Ingrid Bergman and Humphrey Bogart, examining in great detail how the tragic love story was told. Suddenly, I remembered the link the Americans had made between the Englishman in uniform and *An Officer and a Gentleman*. I also realized the story of how we met followed a similar pattern to the romantic film. I wondered if, at last, I might be brave enough to write a story based on how I met my Englishman. But, as usual, I got sidetracked and wrote a spy thriller, *The Red King of Helsinki,* instead!

My Blog and The English Heart

My *An Officer and a Gentleman* story had to wait until I started blogging in 2007. And even then it all happened a little by accident. When my readers asked why I came to live in the UK, I began telling the story of how I met my Englishman at the British Embassy in Helsinki. I intended to write just a few posts, but when the story ran and ran, and when I was on entry number 25, I realized I was writing a longer, partly fictional, story. Years, and many, many edits later the novel, *The English Heart,* was finally published in 2013.

The other books in the series came about when readers wanted to know more of Kaisa and Peter's story. I resisted for years writing the sequel, but once I began writing *The Faithful Heart*, it was as if the floodgates had been opened! *The Good Heart* took just months to write, as did the prequel novella, *The Young Heart.* (If you sign up to my mailing list, you will get a free ebook copy of the novella. Go to www.helenahalme.com to find out more). The last novel in the series was a little trickier to write. *The True Heart,* Book 4, came out the fall of 2017. In 2018, I added one final chapter to the Nordic Heart series with a seasonal novella, *The Christmas Heart*.

Sometimes getting inspired takes time, so don't rush this part of the process.

Photos, letters and emails

Use photos, letters, and emails for inspiration.

I was lucky that we'd kept all the letters from our long-distance relationship. They were very useful when I wrote all the books in *The Nordic Heart* series.

I also used old photographs to remind myself of how I felt at the time. I stuck a few chosen ones on the wall in my study for inspiration.

But don't worry if you haven't got any personal items. Just looking at old photos in newspaper archives may jog your memory and give you inspiration. Or seeing an item in a jumble sale may bring old emotions to the surface. Anything from the relevant time will be useful to you.

Music, films and other arts

As well as images and items, music and other arts can be very evocative too. To get inspired, listen to the bands and artists of the era. Remind yourself what films, plays, art exhibitions you saw then. Or books you read at the time and how those informed your decisions and beliefs. Seeing an old film or a painting can evoke important, strong, memories.

Get some distance

Often when you are physically removed from a place, or people, it's easier to see them fully, and to describe them well.

I write about my childhood events and places, as well as about a love story which took place some 30 years ago. When I'm traveling back home, or even to a new country, I get inspired to write and make copious notes. I don't think there's been one trip where I haven't thought of a new twist or a new plot line to a story. Often I get inspired to write a completely new novel and start one. Some of these ideas stick, some don't. But all of them are in my notebooks to be picked up when I'm short on inspiration.

What was it like back then?

Research the era thoroughly; you'll be surprised how much you will have forgotten what life was like. You will have forgotten, for example, that Google only started its search engine in 2006, and that only ten years ago, it was unusual to surf the net with your phone. Make sure that you become an expert in the era you are describing. Adding a few pointers about the lack of the internet, for example, if your story is set in the 80s or 90s is a good idea.

Go professional with your research

Use sites like Wikipedia to research the year (or years) in question. This way you can use any political developments, current affairs, sports events or significant artistic happenings as a backdrop to your story. Or you can use libraries to read old newspapers and magazines.

Make sure that if there were some large political events, such as an important election, you include that in your story. Any weather phenomenon, like floods, forest fires, or a particularly hot summer, is also good to add for period color.

Have a look at what TV, film, music, theatre and other arts were popular at the time. Who were the celebrities newspapers wrote about? Who were the most revered or hated political figures?

For example, if in years to come, I'd write about the year 2016, my characters would need to refer to the Brexit vote in the UK, or the election of Donald Trump as US president. I'm sure none of the books written about year 2020 can escape the coronavirus pandemic. These are large world events, which the majority of people know about. They will make your story more authentic.

ACTION POINTS

- Gather all material you have on your life story including photographs, letters and cards – whatever bits and pieces of your life you have saved
- Research the era: what was the weather

like, who was famous and what were the major political or cultural developments during the years you are writing about.

- Read old newspapers and magazines
- Listen to the music of the time. Music can be very evocative and will remind you of how you felt at the time
- Rewatch films of the time, or re-read novels that you loved during that era
- Always make notes, wherever you are!

2

GENRE: WHAT IS THE STORY YOU WANT TO TELL?

In order for your readers to know what type of story they are going to find inside the covers of your book, you need to know what genre your story falls into.

Romance, Spy Thriller or Nordic Noir?

It may be obvious *to you* what the story you want to tell is.

You may, however, be surprised by how many people think they know what they want to write about, but when it comes to it, all their thoughts are jumbled up and they can't decide where to start or how to proceed.

When I was trying to write *The English Heart,* I did know that the central story was the love affair between myself and my Englishman. But there were so many other issues (plot lines) involved in the tale.

We met during the Cold War in a country friendly with the Soviet Union (as Russia was called then). He was a newly qualified Naval Officer, who'd been warned about Russian honey traps. I was engaged to be married to someone else!

Was my story going to be a romance, a spy thriller, or even a Nordic Noir drama?

The romance genre, like all genres, has its own rules. The story centers on the love story, the characters, and their feelings. For the most part, romance novels end happily ever after, after some major difficulties have been overcome by the protagonists. The pace of the story isn't as fast as it is in, say, a thriller.

My story fitted perfectly for the romance genre, because, dear reader, I married him.

This meant that all the other sub-plots had to be reflected back to the love story. The Cold War is still a central theme in the book, but the love story between Kaisa and Peter is the main plot of the novel.

It's important from the very start to know what genre your book falls into.

Main genres

So what are the various genres? There are many, but fiction books can be divided into just five *main* categories.

- Romance
- Mystery, Thriller & Suspense
- Science Fiction & Fantasy
- Teen & Young Adult
- Literary fiction

All these main genres have a multitude of sub-genres, with layers and layers of categories underneath them. Just look up BISAC Subject Codes where book categories are listed, and you'll find there are several to choose from. But when planning the story of your life, it's useful to keep in mind these five main types.

To help you decide what type of story your novel is going to be, it's good to drill a little further into the story and your motivation for wishing to write it.

What Do You Want to Write?

What kind of story do you want to write? Or, even, what kind of books do you enjoy reading? I'd love to write Nordic Noir thrillers, but every time I try to write one, it turns into something else. I love reading romance books too, as long as they are not too sugar-coated.

My very favorite stories are 'mashup' novels, similar to the film (and subsequent TV series) Fargo. Authors who have stretched the Romance genre into more 'Fargoesk' genre are Liane Moriarty and Elin Hilderbrand. These are the authors that inspire my writing.

So, even before writing a word, look at the kind of novels and authors you read, and think about what genre they fall into. Then think if your story would fall into that category, taking into account the points about what kind of story it is and why you want to write it.

What is the plot?

Once you've decided what kind of a story you are writing, look at where you should start and how you wish to finish the story.

A storyline needs a main theme, 'a red thread', running through it with a message to the reader on why you wrote the book. My book is really a long love-letter to my husband. Even though it isn't all true, when writing it, I wanted to show him how much meeting him has changed my life, and how I couldn't live without him. In other words, it is a 'Love Conquers All' type of a story and falls neatly into the Romance genre. Perhaps you'll be writing tale of success against all odds, which might be right for the Literary Fiction category. Or an adventure, which will probably fit into the Mystery, Thriller & Suspense genre, or a coming of age story, right for the Teen & Young Adult category.

The most significant event

For me the way to find what kind of story I was writing, as well as how the narrative was going to unravel, i.e. what the plot was going to be, was to ask myself what the significant event in my life was that I wanted to explore within the novel.

Think of the most important and exciting event in your life, and start thinking about how this event shaped your life. In Doris Lessing's semi-autobiographical novel, *A Proper Marriage,* the significant moment is Martha's realization that her marriage is a terrible mistake. In the 1950s when Lessing wrote the novel, having these kinds of thoughts was quite revolutionary, especially when a small was child involved. *A Proper Marriage* is a Literary Fiction novel. It's also a tale of self-discovery, which includes coming of age, and political awakening.

Change your story

You could also think how an event *could have* changed the path you've taken if you or someone else in the book had acted differently.

Start plotting a scene based on the significant event, changing the conclusion for better or worse, or inventing new plot twists.

For example, in *The English Heart*, I could have made my heroine into a Soviet spy and changed the scene where Kaisa and Peter talk about Russian honey traps. This would have changed the whole genre of the novel from a Romance to a Spy Thriller.

When you've decided which scene you are going to explore and how it's going to go, write a short paragraph about it focussing on how you or someone close to you felt, or would have felt in the changed circumstances.

ACTION POINTS

- What kind of books do you like?
- What genre does your reading fall into?
- Think about why you are writing the story
- What is the theme of your book?
- What kind of novel do you want to write?
- Think about the plot, what is the significant event in the book?
- Try to change something in the 'real' story and write a short scene with the new details

3

PLOT: EXCITING BEGINNING
AND END

Now you've an idea what type of story you are writing, it's time to think about the start of your novel. It needs to have an exciting beginning.

The most central event

What was the most central, critical point of the story? Start there. "She was born in a small village in West of England" may be the truth, but it may be a tad boring and not very unique. (Everyone is born at some point). Now, of course, if you were born on a raft in the middle of the Pacific, that's a different matter.

Reader's eye

Always think how others might view your story. What would you think if you'd told someone their life sounds interesting and the first thing they'd tell you is where they were born. You'd run a mile, thinking the person will be hours telling you his or her story.

At the beginning of Doris Lessing's *A Proper Marriage* we meet Martha when she is at her unhappiest, just as she is deciding to leave her life in colonial Africa behind.

The English Heart is a romance, so it starts when Kaisa meets Peter at the British Embassy in Helsinki. I was lucky in that the meeting place where I met my husband was such a romantic and exclusive place; I can assure you it wasn't what my life was like at all! But naturally I used that setting to the fullest, and tried to make it sound as romantic as possible.

Excite the reader

The start needs to make the reader want to find out more, so don't worry too much about explaining everything – you can add back story later. But make sure you do start at the pinnacle of the story, and not at the beginning of your life.

You can also start a novel with just a statement of fact, (Think Jane Austen's *Pride and Prejudice*), but make sure the statement is linked to the main theme or 'the red thread' running through your novel.

'It is a truth universally acknowledged, that a single man in possession of a good fortune must be in want of a wife.'

Austen's novel is a romantic comedy, so the beginning is humorous, it neatly (almost) summarizes the plot and it piques the reader's interest.

Any fiction book needs a beginning and an end, plus an engaging plot. Your life may well have been exciting and unique, but you still need to follow (some of) the general rules of storytelling.

The Five Commandments of Storytelling

As well as finding the start of your story, you need to consider the ending, the structure and shape of the storyline. In other words, you need a narrative arc for your story.

The narrative arc is made up of the events in your story — the sequence of occurrences in the plot — and determines the peaks and plateaus that set the pace. A good arc is vital if you want to engage your readers from start to finish, and deliver a satisfying conclusion.

The Five Commandments of Storytelling is one useful way to chart your story arc. It'll also help you determine the plot of your novel.

1. Inciting Incident

The start of the book, the significant event I spoke about above is often called *The Inciting Incident.* Something has to happen to the protagonist to change his world. For example, a woman who's never been in love meets the man of her dreams when she bumps into him in a park. Perhaps she accidentally pours hot coffee over his pristine, white shirt.

2. Progressive Complications

Complications are crucial in a story, and it's also important that the problems mount up, i.e. become progressive. In my example, the man of her dreams (whose shirt she ruined) is a single dad with three kids. Then she finds out his wife died and he cannot love anyone else as much. And his kids hate him dating anyone else.

3. Crisis

This is the point where our heroine is forced to act. Will she forget about this man she loves and who loves her back? There has to be something, like a job offer on the other side of the world, a discovery that the wife is alive after all, or something to force our loved-up protagonists to make a decision.

4. Climax

This is where the character acts on the final decision, which creates a chain reaction. She moves away and tries to forget about our man or the wife turns out to be a cheating tramp, who, all of this time, has lived a second life with another man in a luxurious villa on a Caribbean island.

5. Resolution

As well as an engaging start, it is crucial that your story has a good ending. The Resolution is where all the threads of the main plot and the side plots are brought together and the book ends. Our couple get together and marry, and the cheating wife ends up alone.

There Are No Rules

A word of warning, however. It's very useful to look at the various aspects of the story to find the arc. But the above example is a very simplistic way of looking at the elements of a novel. I agree with Doris Lessing, who said,

There are no laws for the novel. There have never been, nor can there ever be.

ACTION POINTS

- Think of the most crucial situation in your life's story
- Write a paragraph or two, charting the

scene, making sure you get the raw
emotion of the characters onto the page

- Think about the ending; does it fit the
beginning of the story?
- Chart your story arc along the lines of
The Five Commandments of Storytelling

4

PLOT: TIMELINE OF THE STORY

When turning your life into fiction, it can be very difficult to determine the timeline of the story. You are writing about real events, which probably happened over several years, or even decades. However, in order to write an engaging novel, you need to decide what to include and what to leave out of your story.

Shorten Your Story

Making your story shorter makes the plot more exciting. In real life, events often occur slowly. It's only when you look back that you see the main theme of the narrative and what significance singular events had on your life – and to the plot of your book.

Shortening the time-frame is one way of making the story more concise and interesting, however this isn't the only way you can make the plot move faster.

If your story takes place over a lifetime, for example, you need to find the most exciting and crucial points (see The Five Commandments of a Storytelling in the previous chapter). If you limit these two, three or four events, which make your main protagonist's life increasingly difficult and complicated, your story will suddenly begin to take shape.

Gaps in the storyline

In order to achieve this, you can leave gaps, even years between chapters. In this case, it might make sense to title the chapters with the date and/or place, 'Autumn 1988', 'Helsinki 1979' or similar, so that the reader can easily see that the timeline has moved on. It's easy for the reader to pick up the thread of the story again, especially if little of relevance happened during the intervening period.

Or you can transpose the events into a completely new, shorter timeframe, or even into the future, and write a dystopian fantasy novel. The world (of books and genres) is your oyster!

No irrelevant plot points, please

Another way of shortening the story is to leave out irrelevant plot points.

It's a difficult call to decide what is relevant and what's less important to the story line, but if you keep to three or four high points in your plot, this should make it easier to choose what to include and what to omit.

In addition to moving the plot forwards, some events – or scenes – may be needed in the narrative, just to show the character traits of the main protagonists.

Ask yourself, 'Does this detail take the story further?' or 'Is this detail essential in describing the character(s)?' If the answer is 'No' to both of these questions, then you can leave the event, scene, or detail out.

Don't forget, your aim is to keep the interest of the reader piqued.

I'd recommend that, initially, you are very selective with the events that go into your book. You can always add plot twists, or story points later, if the story needs it or if they are necessary to make your characters more multifaceted.

Chronology

Chronology is also a very important consideration. The usual way of describing events is in the time line that they occurred, ie, day by day, or month by month.

But you can, of course, write the book in a non-chronological order. This is a very difficult to get right, but there are some talented authors who do this brilliantly. Perfect examples of this type of storytelling can be found in Margaret Atwood's *The Blind Assassin* or Kate Atkinson's *Life After Life.*

Two timelines

Changing the chronology of your book will work wonderfully if, for example, the main event needs a lot of backstory for it to become relevant for the reader. In *Coffee and Vodka*, a novel loosely based on my early life, the experiences of the main protagonist as a child are crucial to the plot. On the advice of one of my MA in Creative Writing tutors, I divided the novel into two parallel timelines.

As well as dealing with a long timeline, this method also creates further tensions. You are essentially telling two separate stories, each with their own plots and arcs. The reader is spurred on to find out how the two stories fit together as well as wishing to find out what happens in each timeline.

The way I achieved this was by writing both stories in 'normal' chronological order first. Then I printed out the chapters and placed them in an order that made sense. (I put all the chapters on the floor and physically rearranged them). Once I had the new order, I edited the book to make sure the story flowed from one era to the next. I repeated this process many times before handing the manuscript to my editor.

Writing your story in a chronological order is much simpler than mixing the time order. However, as you can see from my example with *Coffee and Vodka*, jumping from the past to the present is not as difficult as you may first think.

ACTION POINTS

- Make a list of the main events in your life – or the story arc of the book
- Put these into a chronological order (if this is how you wish to write your novel)
- Decide which ones *have* to be included in the novel, and put the others aside in a file for you to pick up later if needed for characterization
- Try writing two timelines and joining the two stories after you've written the first draft

5

POINT OF VIEW

Choosing the point of view for your life story is critical. It will determine the feel of the story and will indicate the genre of your book to the reader.

First person point of view

The first point of view narrative is a very personal one. It's often used by novelists who want the reader to get close to the protagonist. In *The Memoirs of a Geisha*, Arthur Golden uses first person narrative so convincingly that many people, when the novel was published, were fooled into thinking that a Japanese woman had written the book.

The first point of view can feel very intimate to the reader and can make a work of fiction feel like a memoir.

Third person point of view

Conversely, however, when you are writing your life story, you may wish the book to appear more like a work of fiction, and not a memoir.

When you use your own life as the plot, the novel could seem too personal, and too much like an autobiography, with a first-person narrative.

In this case, using the third person point of view may be more suitable.

When I wrote *The English Heart* blog posts, I did use first person, but later when I began editing the novel, I decided to change the whole story into third person. This way the novel became more of a fictional account and sounded less like a memoir. This was advice given to me by one of my early readers, and I am eternally grateful for her comments.

Both or omniscient

Some authors use both third and first person narratives together, and this is a technique to consider especially when writing a story based on your own life. Again, it isn't an easy technique to get right, but if you are writing from several points of view, it is an excellent way to distinguish the different voices.

Another alternative is to use omniscient narrative – a narrative in third person which has all all-knowing perspective, which includes hidden truths and secrets the characters hold from each other. This can work well in fiction, especially if you do not wish to tell the story from one point of view in particular. Or cannot choose which character should be the main protagonist.

But beware.

Since your aim is to write a piece of fiction based on your own life, and the omniscient narration assumes the author him or herself is speaking, the novel can sound a lot more like an autobiography rather than fiction. Just as with first person narrative, this point of view may be too personal for a fictional story of your life.

Several points of view

If your story includes several different protagonists' stories and/or you are not comfortable with using an omniscient voice, you could try telling the story from two or more characters' points of view.

Using voices of several people gives a story depth. It allows you, the writer, to explain the characters' motivations and problems by allowing the reader to look inside their minds. It enables you to dig deeper into the main protagonists' feelings and personality.

Using several points of view in a novel also allows you to create tension. For example, if a plot point is known by one character and not the other, the reader feels they have more information about the protagonists, and feel more invested in the story.

When I rewrote *The English Heart,* compiling the blog posts into a novel, I added Peter, the male voice, into the novel. This made it easier for me to explain certain plot points that Kaisa, the main character, found out about later. Peter's point of view also allowed me to explain his frustrations within the relationship. Using two points of view helped to explain why Kaisa and Peter struggled to communicate their true feelings to each other.

ACTION POINTS

- Decide on who's point of view you are going to use – are you going to write using just the one, or the voices of several characters in your book
- Are you going to use an omniscient point of view?
- Think about using third person narrative throughout to make the book seem more fictional
- Try using first person narrative for the main protagonist (you), and third person for the other main character(s)

6

STRONG CHARACTERS

When you decide to turn your life into fiction, determining which characters to include, on the face of it, seems a simple task. However, once again, you must remember that your story needs to entertain the reader. Therefore, you must make sure that your characters are complicated and interesting. I'm not saying that your life is filled with boring people, but in order to make a story fly, it needs strong characters.

Know your characters

In order to create strong and complicated characters for your life story, you need to know the people you are writing about really, really well. I mean, you need to know them inside out.

'What? But I do know these people really, really, well!' you say.

But do you know them well enough to write about them? You may know exactly how they look, talk, walk, what makes them happy, angry, or sad. But do you know their innermost wishes? The demons that wake them up in the middle of the night? Do you know what motivates them?

When using characters that you already are intimately acquainted with in a novel, it's useful to treat them as if you didn't know them at all and chart their likes, dislikes, and motivations as if you were making them up. This allows you to analyze them more rationally and gives you the tools to write about them more lucidly.

Treating your real people as characters also gives you some distance from the story and allows you to write a narrative that makes sense to the reader.

Analyzing your characters in detail, as if they were unknown to you, will, in turn, let you get under their skin and make the story colorful and gripping.

Analyze your characters

To analyze your characters, use a list (see below) for each one of them. You can add a few details, or leave some out.

It all depends on the type of story you are writing. If your story is a Romance, it's more important to know the emotional side of all the main protagonists than it is in, for example, a crime thriller.

So before you start, as well as the character, think about the story. Consider which of the character's personality traits impact the story, and emphasize those. You can ignore any attributes that do not fit plot, or exaggerate some, or add a few that do not exists 'in real life'.

In my novel *The English Heart*, Peter's two main passions are his career in the Royal Navy, and his fear of failure in the same. He loves Kaisa and wants what's best for her, but not to the detriment of his dream of a brilliant future in the submarine service. His ambition makes him often put his career first instead of their relationship.

In real life, my husband isn't like that at all. Yes, when younger and serving in the Navy, he was ambitious, but it didn't overpower him in the same way as it does Peter. It wasn't his *raison d'être* as it is Peter's in the whole of *The Nordic Heart Series*.

List of character traits

Here is the list of character traits that I use when plotting a new novel or series:

- Role in the novel
- Personality
- Appearance
- Job/Occupation
- Main passion in life
- Character Flaw(s)
- Motivation in life/in the story
- Deep beliefs
- Deep fears (never uttered)
- Dislikes
- Likes

- Loves
- External Conflicts

Leave out characters

When writing a book about your own life, it's easy to add all the people that you know or knew. But having too many characters in a novel can be confusing for the reader. They can can make the story unnecessarily complicated and jarring.

Although an obvious masterpiece, Tolstoy's *War and Peace* is a difficult read due to the vast cast of characters.

Having a smaller number of people will also increase the pace of the novel, which in turn will make it more enjoyable for the reader.

Try not to include every real person in your novel.

To cut down your 'cast', make a list of all the people in your story, in the order of importance, with their roles in the novel. You'll soon discover if there are characters that you can drop.

Combine characters

If, however, leaving out people from your life story seems impossible, or there are still too many in the book, try combining characters.

Merging two or more real people into one character will make them more complicated and in this way, stand out in the story. It's well known that the more enigmatic and difficult a character is, the more enjoyable reading about them is.

Unusual attributes

Each one of the characters in your book must stand out, so if you can't help having two similar people in your cast, try giving one some unusual attributes. An accent, a difference in their physical appearance, sexual orientation or even disability will make them more memorable to the reader.

ACTION POINTS

- Fill in the list above for each character
- Make a list of all the characters and see if you can cut the 'cast' down

- Think of two or three people that could be combined into one, complicated character, and include them in a scene
- See which plot points could involve the same characters, rather than several different ones
- Add different attributes to characters so that readers know who's who

7

DYNAMIC DIALOGUE

Dialogue is a literary technique where two or more characters are engaged in conversation with one another. In a novel, it's the oil that lubricates the cogs of the story to turn. When I was younger, I'd sometimes skip whole sections of a book just to jump to the dialogue. I did this especially if the book was gripping, and I needed desperately to find out what happens next.

Dialogue or narrative?

Narrative, on the other hand, can be defined as a report of related events presented to readers, in words arranged in a logical sequence.

Deciding when to use dialogue, as opposed to narrative, is a difficult judgment to make. A good novel should have both of these elements of fiction. Dialogue makes a scene more dramatic, but if a book has too much dialogue, this can make it seem odd, and will soon turn some readers off the novel.

It can also be difficult for the reader to concentrate on who is speaking, or who said what. I tend to just know when I have to place some dialogue into the text, so my advice is that you tell the most interesting points of the plot in dialogue, and the rest in the narrative form. But it's all a question of balance.

Dialogue in novels isn't 'real'

So we've determined that dialogue is very important in a story. But how do you make dialogue gripping and realistic to the reader?

Some think that recounting the words that they have overheard or witnessed is the best way to write exciting scenes. Sadly, this is far from the truth. If you've ever listened to people on the bus – or even better – recorded a real conversation, you will find that people tend to take a long time to say what they mean. People use a lot of unnecessary comments, such as 'Hmm, 'What I mean is', 'Really', 'Aha'. They also repeat themselves and often jump from one topic to the next without any warning whatsoever.

In a novel, even though the dialogue is the most exciting part, it needs to be measured. The fewer words a character uses, the more weight they carry. On the other hand, adding a few buts and ifs, for example, will change the expressions dramatically. So be very selective with your dialogue. Pepper it throughout the book as if it was some kind of exotic spice. Too little and the novel is bland, too much and it's unreadable.

Informative dialogue

As well as the spice in your book, dialogue also has several important purposes in the story.

Firstly, dialogue should be informative. Words spoken by the characters should move the story along by telling the reader what someone is thinking or doing.

Look at the statement, 'I love you'. It's powerful. It tells the reader that the character has deep feelings, or at least he or she wants the other person to believe that they have sincere intentions.

Show character's attributes and motivation

Secondly, dialogue should show both the relationship between characters, but also the speaker's own inner and outer conflicts.

Having a conflict in a dialogue is often necessary to exhibit the relationship between the characters. If the protagonist says, 'But I love you!' the sentence conveys the desperation of the character. Here, the 'I love you' sentiment is more a plea for empathy. The reader understands that the person speaking those words may have another motive than simply declaring his love.

I hope you can see from these two examples how the reader learns a lot about the character's motivations through the dialogue you put into their mouths.

We rarely say what we mean

Something which is true both in real life and in novels is that people and characters rarely say exactly what they mean. In the above example, our protagonist is more likely to say, 'You mean a lot to me', or 'Your scarf is exactly the same color as your eyes.' They may even say (or shout) the complete opposite, 'I hate you!' Love and hate are closely aligned emotions, so a character may well say the latter but mean the former.

When you are writing dialogue for a novel based on real-life, you need to think carefully about what to include and what to leave out. Instead of thinking of the words the people used, think about what they wanted to convey with those words. Or what they would say while meaning something completely different. Cut out unnecessary words and remember that dialogue is the exotic spice in your novel.

Who is speaking?

Finally, it may seem obvious that the reader needs to know who is speaking the words in your dialogue. But you'd be surprised how blind us writers can be to this type of error. Because we know the story, characters, and plot intimately, we often forget that the reader isn't as knowledgeable about our novel. My editor often picks out dialogue where I haven't made it clear who the words on the page belong to. So please always make it clear to the reader who is speaking.

The most important point is not to use real dialogue, and to make sure the dialogue informs the reader of the character's inner thoughts, and moves the story on.

ACTION POINTS

- Make a list of the most important points in your story and see how dialogue would work in the scenes
- Make sure your dialogue moves the story on
- Ensure that there's conflict in each scene with dialogue
- Make sure the relationships between the characters in each scene shine through in your dialogue

- Make sure the reader always knows who is speaking
- Don't use real life dialogue in your book – cut, cut, and cut!

8

WRITE WITH CONFIDENCE

I've talked a lot about what you should *not* do and what you should think about when turning your life story into fiction. Admittedly, when writing fiction, there are a lot of things to consider.

You have a story to tell

But you should not feel overwhelmed by all the advice I've dispensed in the previous pages. What you should remember is that the biggest problem most writers have is inspiration.

If you've made it this far in my book, you have a story to tell. A tale that you are inspired to write.

And inspiration is the biggest gift of all for a writer.

So don't worry about letting your pen fly when you start writing. Don't worry about the genre, whether the beginning is exciting enough, about the timeline, characters or what the dialogue looks like at this stage. These are details you can fix later. I'd say the only thing you have to decide is whose point of view you are going to use. But even this can be changed in the editing process!

I find it very useful to write a small passage from the viewpoint of each of the main characters and choose the one that one feels the most comfortable. You might be surprised by your own reaction. When writing your own life story, it's often easier to write someone else's viewpoint first and add your own later.

You may find that since you know the plot – and the characters (if you've already analyzed them as I showed you in Chapter 6) , writing the novel can be very quick. If you decide later to change scenes, plot or tweak your characters, that's easy.

Another tip is to forget about the 'truth'. I find that if I don't worry too much about how closely aligned the story is with real life, my writing becomes much more fluid and confident. In all the books where I've used my own life as inspiration, the 'true' story is only a framework to the novel.

Write Regularly

The most important thing you can do at this stage is to write regularly. Try to at least *look* at your manuscript once per day, and if you can get a few words down at the same time, so much the better. Even if you just do a few edits every day, this keeps the story and the characters fresh in your mind and makes it easier to sit down and write some more.

Think of writing as physical exercise; the longer you leave it, the more difficult it is to get going again.

Blog

One way to ensure you write regularly, is to start a blog. You can do this anonymously, which makes it easier to write about your own life. Blogs are not as fashionable today as they were when I began writing one in the early 2000s, but they are still a hugely useful tool for writers. And you never know, if you learn how to use Search Engine Optimization (SEO), you may gain a useful audience by blogging, ready for when your book is published.

I wrote the first version of *The English Heart* as a series of posts. I'm not sure I would have ever told the story had I not received such a lot of encouragement from the readers of my blog, and from other bloggers. These wonderful people spurred me on to eventually edit the posts and write a novel.

The two blogging platforms I would recommend are WordPress and Blogger. Both are free, easy to use, and have ready-made blogging communities that you can engage with. But there are many more platforms out there. You could even write short posts using Twitter, Instagram, or submit chapters to online communities such as Wattpad.

If you have the money and time, setting up a website with a blog attached is the best solution, as it ensures that you alone own the copyright to your blog. And later on, when you have several published books under your belt, a website is a good platform to have where you can market your books directly and promote your writer profile.

I'm old-fashioned and love blogging, so even if many other authors have stopped the practice to save more time for writing, I still try to put out a post at least once per month. (You can find my blog on www.helenahalme.com/blog/) .

Writing prompts

To get motivated, it's also worth while investigating online writing programs. Some of them are designed to speed up your writing, such as the National Novel Writing Month. NaNoWriMo as it's known, happens every November and has a community of over 400,000 writers around the world who undertake to write 50,000 words in a month. You update and share your progress with your chosen friends each day, and get badges & other encouragements from the community. This is great fun, and each time I've taken part, the process has produced a novel.

When it's not November, NaNoWriMo online community provides writing prompts on its

Twitter feed, which are incredibly useful if, for example, you are in a difficult phase in your story.

There are many other sites and meet-up programers out there. Some are local and some are online. It's worth investigating the ones nearest to you, especially if you are confident enough to go and write together in a cafe or library with other people (I wasn't for many, many years!). If not, check out Twitter and Facebook for groups that encourage you to write.

Free Writing

Another way to release your creative juices is to write fast, using something called f-r-e-e-writing. Orna Ross speaks about this process of allowing your mind to wander while you write for a few minutes in her *Go Creative* books.

This is a technique I've used on several occasions, so I heartily recommend it!

The Occasional Writer

If you can't commit to a daily routine, you could try writing in spurts. Many authors do this. They go on a retreat, or allow themselves a few weeks or months each year to complete a book. I tend to find it easier to write a little every day, be it writing for my blog, nonfiction or fiction. For many people, it's not possible to devote time every day because of work and/or family commitments. Some writers also find it easier to live in the book for an intense period, rather than flip in and out of real life and fiction while completing the novel.

Turn off your inner critic

When you are writing your first draft, it's important to turn off your inner critic. It's rumored that Ernst Hemingway said, 'The first draft of anything is rubbish.' Whether it was him or someone else, it's a good sentiment to remember when you are writing. Nobody ever has published the first draft of their book.

No-one. Ever.

I have covered in the previous chapters how to think about telling your life story. I've encouraged you to go professional with your research and decide on the genre of your story. I've advised you to have an exciting beginning and end, as well as consider the timeline and point of view. I've urged you to make your characters engaging and complicated, and to use dynamic dialogue.

BUT

It is also very important that you do not let all the technical issues stop you from writing. Particularly if the central character is you, don't hold back, just write how you felt, explaining your emotions as if talking to a friend.

The most important thing is that you write with confidence, be it a little every day or intensively for a few weeks at a time.

ACTION POINTS

- Find a point in your day, week, month when you have time to write. I know writers who have given up TV, or wake up an hour earlier in the morning to write
- Start a blog with your story, or submit a chapter each week to Wattpad, or on your website
- Decide to write every day for a month.

Take part in something like NaNoWriMo,
other online or local writing group. If you
can't commit to a month, decide to write
for for just half an hour, every day

- Try 'f-r-e-e-writing' exercises where you
just write what comes into your mind for
five or ten minutes on one subject,
without any censoring any of your
thoughts or the text. (Sometimes it's
better to do this by hand rather than
computer.) You'll be surprised what
comes out!

- Try out a writing retreat, or just spend a
holiday writing. You may be one of those
who find it easier to write intensively for
a few weeks, rather than regularly
every day

- Turn off your inner critic and just, write,
write, and write.

9

SEEK PERMISSION

This chapter is one that I get the strongest reaction to when I talk about turning your life into fiction. Some laugh at the suggestion that while writing a story about your own life, you should seek permission from those that 'appear' in the novel. While others have an aha moment. They realize that it is this that has been stopping them from realizing the dream of writing about their own life. The thought that someone special to them is going to be upset by their words, or that they're going to reveal too much of themselves in the novel, is so scary that they cannot even start writing the story.

What will people think?

I must admit that the question, 'What will people think', was something I very much struggled with too. Worrying about what people close to me might make of my novel(s) was the reason why I didn't start writing until I'd hit my 40s. I don't usually like to think back and regret something I've done or not done, but this is one fact that I'm very much annoyed with myself about.

It wasn't until I realized that letting the person closest to me, my husband, read the chapters as I wrote them solved the issue for me.

Get the main character to read your work

If you are struggling with the same issue about wondering what people will make of your book, think about getting permission to publish from the significant person – or persons – in your story. This is important especially if they can be easily recognized. (And you care about what they think).

Changing the story slightly, combining characters and moving the time-line, will work to eliminate most of the issues with recognition, but if the story is particularly unique to you, it is likely that many people will recognize – or think they recognize – themselves in your story.

You'd be surprised how many people ask me about what is true and what is fiction in my books. I always tell them that all of it is fiction, or if I want to tease them, I say, 'It's for me to know and for you to find out.'

If there are people that you worry about, give your manuscript to them and simply ask for permission to publish. You can give them the whole of the book, or just the parts that concern them.

I found that the best way to seek permission for *The English Heart*, was to let my husband read the chapters *before* I published them on my blog. As a result, he now reads all of my fiction before it goes to my first editor. Nowadays it's more to do with the quality of the text than any approval (see next chapter about editing your book).

Legal considerations

In addition to seeking verbal approval, to make publishing your story less painful on an emotional level, I do believe it's best to protect yourself legally too.

I am not a lawyer, but I believe that if you have fictionalized the story, and made the characters as unrecognizable as you can, you can add a sentence or two to protect yourself at the end of the book. **I repeat, I am not a lawyer and I do not provide this as any form of legal advice**, which I am in no position to provide, but you could try something like this:

All characters and events featured in this book are entirely fictional and any resemblance to any person, organization, place or thing living or dead, or event or place, is purely coincidental and completely unintentional.

Large corporation and official bodies

If there are any parts in your book that could be considered libelous, please do be careful. Without thinking about it, you may write negatively about a large corporation, or official bodies as well as people you know. When one of my books went to my editor, she noticed I'd mentioned something negative about a large computer firm. To get around this, I changed the name of the company to a fictitious one. It pays to be careful because you never know how sensitive large corporations are.

It may be more difficult to change the names of official bodies, so please, please be careful about libelous comments against, say the Post Office, or the Police. It's always worthwhile making up a street name, or some other identifying details so that you don't end up writing something bad about an actual employee of an organization. And naturally, do change their names too!

ACTION POINTS

- Make a list of people who you might be concerned about your book
- Decide if you want to let them read the whole manuscript or just the parts where they are featured

- Make sure you mention the fictitious nature of your book
- Take legal advice if you are at all worried about libelous content in your book

10

EDIT, EDIT, EDIT

Yay! You've made it to the final chapter!

And if you are considering editing your novel, you've made it to the end of your first draft, which is just brilliant. Congratulations!

Edit, edit, edit, and then edit some more

For many writers (me included) the editing phase of writing a novel is the absolute worst one. But others relish this stage. It is satisfying when you have a full manuscript in front of you – words that you alone have written. A story that you have carefully crafted, with characters you have molded and nurtured into being, with a great plot that you have devised and are thrilled with.

What could be sweeter than to make the manuscript even better, sharper and more engaging for the reader?

So, even if I hate it, I am a firm believer in the editing process. I've lost count of how many versions of *The English Heart* (or any of the other books I've published), I've written. I think it's safe to say that there were at least ten drafts before I let anyone near the manuscript.

With time, the editing process does get shorter. With experience, it's easier to spot the weaknesses in the text, characters and plot, and the number of drafts you have to write gets smaller.

All writers follow a different process. If you are meticulous about planning your work well before writing even one word of the manuscript, you are likely to have an easier time editing it. But this doesn't always follow – you may have got two thirds down the story when you discover a huge hole in the plot, or your realize that two of the characters are virtually the same person. Or that the setting is completely wrong for the story. It happens.

So there are no rules on how many versions of the manuscript you need to produce before handing it to a professional editor. As long as you have done all you can for the story and the manuscript is the best possible you can produce, it's time to let it go.

Employ a professional editor

Even though you yourself know exactly what you want to say, sometimes you can lose the meaning of the book in the writing of it. This is when a good editor comes in.

Editing is a professional job. You *can* edit your book yourself. There is a lot of information online (look first on The Alliance of Independent Authors site), but I would advise against doing so, even if you are an editor yourself.

The reason is simply that it's difficult to see the wood for the trees. When you have been working on a manuscript for months, even years, you can lose your ability to see the mistakes in it.

A professionally trained editor, or even just another experienced author, can cast their eye over the work and give you an opinion on what needs to be changed. This first process can also be done by so called Beta Readers, people who like your work and are willing to read first copies of the manuscript.

I use first, Beta Readers, to give me suggestions on the plot and characters, and then send the work to my editor who will, depending on the state of the manuscript suggest more changes, or just do a light edit, pointing out inconsistencies in characterizations or plot.

If this is your first book, I'd spend as much as you can afford on editing the work. You've invested a lot of time on the manuscript, why not make it the best it can possibly be?

Readers are not forgiving; they will spot any mistake or problem with the plot or characters. Robert McKee, the Hollywood script-writing guru says: 'The audience is not only amazingly sensitive, but as it settles into a darkened theater its collective IQ jumps twenty-five points.' (Robert McKee, *Story*, Methuen Publishing 1999).

The same is true about readers. As soon as they start reading your book, they become your harshest critic and your most avid reader in one. Within the first sentences, a contract forms between you, the writer, and the reader. The reader agrees to accept and enjoy the story, the world you have created, and you agree to give them this enjoyment. You as a writer must, therefore, make sure you do everything in your power to help the reader to suspend disbelief.

Avoid bad reviews

Mistakes in the language, plot, point of view, tense, and so on will break this contract with readers and they will stop reading your book, or worse, write an unfavorable review. Which is harsh, I know.

Before I go on, I must make the point that you cannot please all the people all of the time. Negative reviews happen, however well you have prepared your book for publication. They happen to all writers, be they famous, traditionally published authors, or first-time indie writers.

Some say that one-star reviews give your book authenticity. If all your reviews are glowing, it is doubtful they are all genuine. Are they honest and true reviews, or just your friends who've read your book and want to help you along in your new career? These friends and family will want you to succeed, so they may have their blinkers on. Having a few bad reviews shows potential readers that the book has been read widely, not just by those who know the author.

To insure yourself against too many such reviews, or readers who never get to the end of your book, you must employ a professional editor AND proofreader. And I mean a *professional* editor. As good as your mum, dad, or partner are as first readers, they should not be your editors. It's OK to use people close to you as Beta Readers, but they mustn't take the place of an editor. Ideally, your editor is a stranger or someone with whom you have a professional relationship. There are several different kinds of editors and editing.

Different Types of Editors

There are three kinds of editing, depending on the stage of your manuscript. If, like me, you use a wide range of readers, including Beta Readers, you probably don't need to use every type of editor.

The Developmental Edit

The first edit is often called the Developmental Edit. This process looks at the major structural issues in a book. Instead of suggesting that an individual sentence is wrong, or a particular scene could be shorter, the editor might suggest wholesale changes to the book that will involve significant rewriting.

A Developmental Edit concerns itself mainly with the plot, the story arc, the characterization, and setting of the manuscript. Could a plot line be added or removed? Could a character be added or removed to help the story move along? Could a passage of prose be turned into dialogue? Does the book have too much backstory, or not enough? Does the manuscript follow the Five Commandments of Storytelling? (See Chapter 3)

The Line Edit

A Line Edit usually follows the developmental edit. Here the editor looks exclusively at the more linguistic areas of the manuscript. These may include the use of clichés, adverbs, filter words, point of view or tense.

A Line Edit addresses the creative content, writing style, and language use at sentence and paragraph level. But the purpose of a line edit is not to comb the manuscript for errors—rather, a line edit focuses on the way you use language to communicate your story to the reader.

The Copy Edit

The last stage of editing is the Copy Edit. It's the final check of the language used in the book and involves grammar, punctuation, spelling, but also changes to words, word order, sentence length, and appearance. It may even include the restructuring or re-ordering of paragraphs.

Although I do recommend that you employ a professional to do a Developmental and a Line Edit, if your funds do not stretch to every stage, this is one you *absolutely cannot skip*. You can use Beta Readers, friends, fellow writers, or even family to comment on your manuscript and let you know if there are any issues with plot or characters, but you cannot use a person who is not a professional editor to do your copy edit. *I cannot emphasize this enough.*

The Proofread

The Proofread is the final look at the manuscript as a novel. This often takes into account the formatting of the book, how the pages, paragraphs and headings are organized, whether they are consistent throughout the book or not. For example, are capital letters and italics used consistently? Is the text in the right place, ie are the margins the same size across the book? Finally, the proof editor should pick up any minor errors that might have been overlooked by the copy editor.

As you can see, even after you have completed your work on the manuscript, there is still much to be done before you can send it to the printers or publish it online as an eBook. Furthermore as an indie author, I know that having a well-edited, clean copy of my book, with a story that keeps the readers' attention and characters who are complicated and authentic, is just the entry fee to the publishing marketplace.

It is vital, therefore, to have at least one, if not several readers, and a professional editor to proofread your work before you publish it.

Don't change the core of the story

When you work with an editor, there are certain things to remember.

An editor is a professional, but she or he doesn't have the final say. While accepting an editor's word on things like grammar and spelling, it's important to ensure that you protect the core of your book.

When I worked with my editor on *The English Heart*, I was very zealous about retaining the essence of the novel. The novel had to remain as the true love story between an English naval officer and a Finnish student, with the obstacles they faced in order to sustain their long-distance relationship.

You must protect the main theme, or 'red thread', running through your story; the reason you began writing the book in the first place. Always remember to keep your mind on what the book is about, even during the editing process.

It's also always advisable to mark early reviews copies with 'unedited copy' which saves the author's blushes. And of course it's not uncommon to have a few misspelled words in a finished book. Such mistakes are often found even in traditionally published works – more often than in indie books, I find. These days all publishing houses are struggling to keep within their tight budgets. But to have ten or more misspelled words, in my mind, is unforgivable.

Besides, having to correct the manuscript when it's been turned into an eBook and print-ready files is a pain and delays the publishing process unnecessarily.

ACTION POINTS

- Employ a professional line editor
- Make sure you are absolutely clear on what your book is about to ensure your

story remains intact when working with
an editor

- Employ a professional proofreader and
  Beta Readers to read your work before
  publishing
- Mark first review copies with 'unedited
  copy' to save your blushes when spelling
  mistakes are found

OVER TO YOU

This is it! You now have the tools to write your life story. Whether it is a story of your family, of what happened to you or to someone close to you, all you have to do is to 'Apply the seat of your pants to the seat of your chair and start typing.' This is another famous comment attributed to Ernest Hemingway, but whoever said it, there is a great deal of truth in the saying.

The only way your story is going to be written is for you to start writing it. And keep going at it. It doesn't matter how long it takes, how little you write each day, week or even month, as long as you keep going.

I hope I've been able to help you a little with the process of telling your life story. Following the ten steps above, I'm confident you'll be able to turn your life into a novel. At least it worked for me!

A FREE STORY

You can now sign up to my mailing list and get a free copy of *The Young Heart,* a novella based on a true love story from Finland.

'Wonderfully intimate and honest.' – Pauliina Ståhlberg, Director of The Finnish Institute in London.

Is she too young to fall in love? A standalone read, *The Young Heart* is a prequel to the acclaimed 1980s romance series, *The Nordic Heart.*

Find out more on my website here:
www.helenahalme.com/want-a-free-book-2/

ACKNOWLEDGMENTS

This is my first non-fiction book. I've previously written academic text, which I used to find very hard to produce because of its restrictions (as you may understand having read this book, I have trouble sticking to the truth).

I did, to my huge amazement, win a prize for my thesis, so I guess I got used to it in the end. I'd like to thank John Nurminen for the award and their encouragement back in 1985 for me to consider writing as a career. It took over two decades for me to finally do it, but hey, better late than never!

I'd also like to thank Joanna Penn and Orna Ross for their tireless encouragement and the work they continue to do for self-published authors.

Finally, I couldn't have written a word without my first, faithful reader, David Frise. As well as a brilliant proofreader, he is a loving husband, my best friend, and an excellent cook, keeping both my mind and body nourished.

ALSO BY HELENA HALME

Coffee and Vodka: A Nordic family drama

The Red King of Helsinki: Lies, Spies and Gymnastics

ABOUT THE AUTHOR

Prize-winning writer, Helena Halme grew up in Tampere, Finland, and moved to the UK via Stockholm and Helsinki in her twenties. She's a former BBC journalist, magazine editor and bookseller.

Since gaining an MA in Creative Writing at Bath Spa University, Helena has published two nonfiction and eleven fiction titles, including six in *The Nordic Heart* series.

As a self-publishing coach, Helena helps other creatives write, publish and market their books. On her new website, www.selfpublishingcoach. co.uk, she shares more of her writing tips.

CONTENTS

COPYRIGHT

Made in the USA
Columbia, SC
12 April 2023